DIGITAL AND INFORMATION LITERACY ™

GRAPHIC DESIGN AND DESKTOP PUBLISHING

JOAN OLECK

rosen publishing's
rosen central™

New York

*To Anya, 14, who already knows more
about graphic design than I ever will*

Published in 2011 by The Rosen Publishing Group, Inc.
29 East 21st Street, New York, NY 10010

First Edition

Library of Congress Cataloging-in-Publication Data

Oleck, Joan.
Graphic design and desktop publishing / Joan Oleck. — 1st ed.
   p. cm. — (Digital and information literacy)
Includes bibliographical references and index.
ISBN 978-1-4358-9425-9 (library binding)
ISBN 978-1-4488-0593-8 (pbk)
ISBN 978-1-4488-0606-5 (6-pack)
1. Graphic design (Typography)—Juvenile literature. 2. Desktop publishing—Juvenile
literature. I. Title.
Z246.O45 2011
686.2'2544536—dc22

                                                               2010004841

Manufactured in the United States of America

CPSIA Compliance Information: Batch #S10YA: For further information, contact Rosen Publishing, New York, New York, at 1-800-237-9932.

CONTENTS

INTRODUCTION

Graphic design is the art and science of communicating visual ideas, images, and messages. Graphic designers create the designs for classroom textbooks, Web sites, online publications, maps in public places, and many other items. Examples of graphic design are all around us, from the magazines and newspapers we read to the ads we see on television. Every single example of graphic design involves artistic decisions about typeface, page layout, color, photos, and illustrations. Designers work hard to capture a student's attention with a textbook design or create a map that will help people get around.

A generation ago, graphic design work was prepared manually on large boards called mechanicals. Back then, text, photos, and illustrations were pasted into an assemblage on large boards, then photographed and printed. Those days are gone. In the mid-1980s, personal computers revolutionized the world of graphic design. Specifically, a technology commonly known as "what you see is what you get," or WYSIWYG, was developed. This technology allowed computers to display content on a screen in such a way that it closely resembled what it would look like when printed. Today's graphic design programs use WYSIWYG technology, enabling designers to easily prepare printer-ready documents.

The term "desktop publishing" refers to people's ability to design and create printed matter themselves. At one time, this was not possible. It took numerous people with different areas of expertise to publish a book, magazine, or advertisement. Today, a personal computer with design and desktop publishing software is all that's needed—plus a designer's imagination and inventiveness. While desktop publishing is typically associated with publication layouts and books, it's a term that extends to billboards, product packaging, and just about any other medium. Graphic design and desktop publishing enable people to design newsletters, flyers, posters, blogs, and Web sites—often at little to no cost.

Chapter 1

Design Basics

Before sitting down to use a computer, most designers quickly sketch some ideas with a pencil and paper. These sketches are called thumbnails. Thumbnails are designs that are created to rough out the main idea for a design. All designs, no matter how complex or ornate, are created from a few basic elements. These basic tools make up the vocabulary of graphic design.

Basic Elements of Design

Focal points, lines, shapes, textures, and forms are some of the basic elements used in the composition of graphic designs. Focal points are used to determine where the person looking at the design will focus. The focal point of the design might be in the center, or it might be off to one side. The composition of the design ultimately determines where the focal point is.

Designers use lines, rules, and space to tell viewers' eyes where to go in a design. Lines can be used to suggest motion or connect two different areas or elements in the design. By using patterns, such as repeating lines or dots, designers can create texture. Texture can give a two-dimensional design a multidimensional feel. Shadows and tone can also give a design the appearance of depth. Tone is the degree, or gradient, of lightness and darkness of one color.

Consider the roles that different shapes play in a design. Imagine creating a newsletter describing a classroom survey on what students think is the best young adult book series. The choices are Harry Potter, Twilight, and Cirque du Freak. A designer creating this newsletter might start with a blank rectangle on his or her computer. After making some thumbnails, the designer would use software tools to create rectangular columns for the text of the newsletter, squares for photos and graphs, and perhaps even a more artistic shape to highlight an image—say, a wizard's cap from Harry Potter.

Today's young designers have an arsenal of computer software tools to help them execute complicated layouts and designs. Beyond technology, human imagination and inventiveness are the real "tools" that create the kinds of designs that capture a viewer's attention.

Hierarchy

Hierarchy refers to the level of status given to each element in a group. Designers decide what the hierarchy of a design will be, then choose which elements of the design will be emphasized. For instance, the more important elements are usually at the top of the page, and the less important elements are usually found toward the bottom. Font size and color choice can also help show hierarchy.

Think about designing that newsletter about the best young adult book series. The newsletter needs a name, which will probably appear in large, bold letters at the top. The main story will appear in regular text that is in a smaller font than the name of the newsletter. The main story should probably

Newspapers illustrate the design concept of hierarchy, with the newspaper name being the largest, boldest element on the page, followed by the day's lead story, located at the top right of the page and topped by a headline.

appear just below the newsletter name and to the right—since English speakers generally look to the right of a printed page first. The story should start with a headline, again in large, bold type (but not as large as the newsletter name). Other stories should be located to the left and below, in slightly smaller type, showing their lower placement in the newsletter's design hierarchy.

Professional graphic designers often work with others to create desktop publishing projects. For instance, designers might work with authors, illustrators, and photographers to create a design. The informational content of a design often determines the hierarchy of its elements. Several design elements can be used to denote hierarchy in a design. These elements are proportion, scale, contrast, and balance.

- Proportion, or scale, describes the relationships between the sizes of various objects in a design. For instance, the headline of a story in a newsletter is larger than the text of the story. Increasing the scale of a design element emphasizes it—the larger a newspaper headline is, the more important the story seems. The scale of a design element might be exaggerated to make a humorous point. For instance, imagine a cartoon for the newsletter that includes gigantic characters from Harry Potter or Twilight looming over an image of the students who voted in the survey.
- Contrast is established when the difference between two elements is visible. For instance, the contrast between the size of an elephant and a Chihuahua is established when the two animals are pictured next to each other. In a black-and-white photograph, adjusting the contrast highlights the dark and light areas.
- Balance describes how elements look on the page. Are these elements symmetrical, meaning equally balanced, or asymmetrical, meaning unbalanced? Asymmetrical compositions can create effective designs by emphasizing certain elements over others.

In a black-and-white photograph, like this one of New York's famed Chrysler Building, a designer can adjust the contrast to emphasize the light and dark areas of the image.

Color

Color is a powerful design tool. Computer design programs focus on one of two color models: the additive color model and/or the subtractive color model. The additive color model uses the colors red, blue, and green (RGB), and the subtractive color model uses the colors cyan, magenta, yellow, and black (CMYK).

How to Put Colors Together

When focusing on what colors to use, designers must first decide what mood or feeling they want to establish. Reds and yellows can give a design a warm look. Blues, purples, and greens can create a cooler, more subdued feel. Complementary colors can lend a feeling of calm to a design. Designers who want to ramp things up and create a more "aggressive" design can choose colors that don't normally go together, or colors that clash. Clashing colors add their own special energy to a design.

Design programs allow designers to use any color they want. However, the way a color displays on a computer monitor is not necessarily the way it will look printed out on a piece of paper. This is because color on a computer screen is created by projected light. However, our eyes see the color of ink on paper because of reflected light. Some professional graphic designers adjust the colors of their design before sending it to the printer so that it will match what they see on the screen. Designers typically consult a swatch book, or a guide to color mixing, such as *Tintbook* or *Postscript Process Color Guide*. These guides are available in both hard copy and digital versions.

RGB

The RGB color model is used to display images on computer monitors and televisions. In the RGB color model, all other colors are made from some combination of red, green, and blue. These three colors can be combined to make any other color on the color spectrum. When all three colors are combined in equal amounts, they create white. When all three colors are absent, the result is black.

Any color made from a combination of these three colors is known as a secondary color. For instance, green, purple, and orange are secondary colors. Tertiary colors are the colors made by mixing red, green, or blue with their adjacent secondary colors on a color wheel. Graphic design and desktop publishing programs such as Adobe Photoshop, Illustrator, and InDesign allow designers to mix colors digitally. These colors can be used to color fonts, as well as to create backgrounds, lines, gradients, and tints.

CMYK

The CMYK color system is a subtractive color model used for printing. This color system works by filtering out additive colors. For instance, imagine a white piece of paper. Remember, white is a combination of red, green, and blue. When different CMYK color inks are printed on the paper, they act as filters, only letting certain additive colors through. These are the colors that the viewer sees. This is why the CMYK color model is known as subtractive color: the inks are used to literally subtract different colors until the designer obtains the color he or she wants.

When a designer wants to print an image, the computer sends it to the printer as a CMYK image. There are other color systems, such as HSB (which stands for hue, saturation, and brightness) and Pantone, which is a copyrighted color system that allows designers to specify colors through a numeric system. However, CMYK is the most common. Examples of CMYK

Modern graphic design and desktop publishing software enables designers to choose from thousands of different colors. Designers can use swatch books like this to aid in the color selection process and confirm with printers what a color will look like when it's printed.

printing are all around. For instance, using a magnifying glass to look at a color image in a magazine will reveal the dots of color that comprise the image, using different percentages of CMYK colors.

Designing, creating, and printing an advertisement or a magazine page once involved a great deal of specialized equipment and usually could not be accomplished by a single person. Today, modern computer software enables a single person to design, lay out, and print—or publish—his or her own work.

Chapter 2

Fonts and Typography

Anyone who has ever used a word processing program knows something about typography. Word processing and design programs allow people to manipulate typography by putting words in italic or boldface and choose from among different fonts.

Most people use one of several common fonts. Some of the most popular are Times New Roman, Arial, Verdana, Georgia, and Helvetica. However, there are thousands of fonts available. Choosing a font is an important step in a design project. Designers need to choose a typeface that suits their audience and the mood they're trying to establish.

Choosing a Typeface

Designers take many factors into consideration before choosing a font. Each font has its own characteristics that make it suitable for different purposes. A font's stylistic details influence its readability and relative degree of seriousness or playfulness.

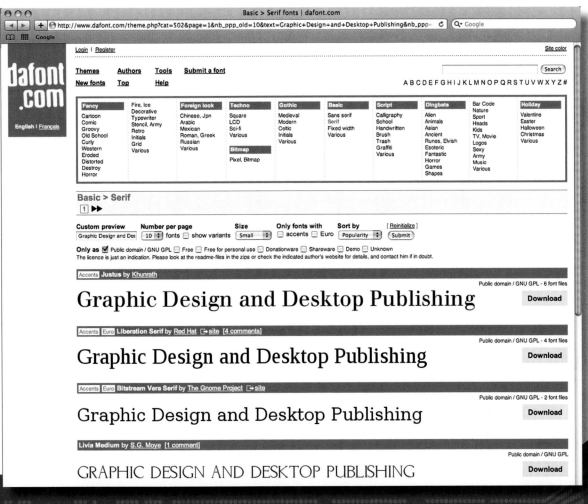

The differences among fonts range from subtle to huge: Does a particular font have serifs, or not? Is it simple and elegant, or is it baroque and decorative? The Web site Dafont.com (http://www.dafont.com) has many public domain fonts available for download.

One consideration is whether or not a font has serifs, which are the little horizontal strokes added to the ends of the lines that form each letter. A font with serifs looks somewhat more traditional compared to a sans serif font without this feature. Sans serif fonts generally look more modern than serif fonts.

When designing a straightforward item like a newsletter, simple type-faces are usually best. A simple typeface will allow people to read a large block of text easily. For designs that require decorative text, such as an invitation to an official reception, a designer may consider using fonts with more stylistic flourishes. For instance, some decorative fonts have swashes, which are like ornate serifs. Ligatures, or typefaces whose letters are pushed together, can produce the look of perfect handwritten script.

Fonts are a key component in showing the hierarchy of a design. Consider the front page of a newspaper: the fonts used in the newspaper's

When choosing fonts, designers consider their use. This airport sign needs to be crystal-clear, as it directs harried passengers to their chosen destination. There's no surprise that a simple, no-nonsense font was chosen for its clarity.

masthead and individual story headlines differ. Different fonts and font sizes can guide the eye down the page, showing readers what to read first. Large font sizes can also come across as more aggressive—in a print advertisement, for example—while small font sizes might be used for the "fine print" at the bottom of the ad. Certain display fonts, such as Caslon Open Face, are specifically designed to be displayed at a large size. This makes them useful for posters and headlines. Font size and style can be used to otherwise break up large blocks of text. For instance, drop caps, or large letters that begin a section of text, can be used to mark the beginning of a new chapter in a book or a new section of a newsletter.

The important thing is for student designers to be careful in their selection of fonts. Not only is it smart to consider the appropriateness of italics, script, or certain flourishes for a particular audience, but it's also smart to think about legibility. Can readers actually read what's been printed? While ornate fonts might look great on an invitation, an entire book printed in an ornate font would be unreadable.

More Typographic Considerations

Designers manipulate the spacing of text by adjusting the leading and kerning. Kerning is the horizontal space between the individual letters of a word. Leading is the vertical spacing between lines of text.

Some programs automatically adjust kerning. For instance, justified text, or text where every line ends at the same place across a page, automatically adjusts the kerning of each line to accomplish this. Advanced graphic layout software enables designers to adjust leading and kerning manually. Manually adjusting the kerning of a block of text can make it contract or expand. If done properly, changes in kerning are usually not usually discernible to readers. Such adjustments make blocks of text less dense. Designers often adjust leading and kerning to make text fit neatly into layouts. In general, such adjustments make blocks of text easier to read.

Before computers became dominant, mechanical typesetting was used to print books, newspapers, and periodicals. A printer had to place each individual letter by hand.

The First Steps

After coming up with preliminary thumbnails for a project, it's time to begin implementing the design. For a newsletter about a survey to determine students' favorite young adult book series, the designer should consider which composition will best convey the information to be presented.

– ☐ X

File   Edit   View   Favorites   Tools   Help

       PRINTERS AND PAPER

Printers and Paper

Desktop publishing software allows anyone to design and publish his or her work. For projects printed at home or school, the choice of printer can make a big difference in the quality of the final product. Inkjet printers generally create better color prints than laser printers, and they're cheaper. The price of inkjet color printers can vary greatly, and different printers have different capabilities.

Some inkjet printers are intended for use on specific kinds of paper. Cheap paper will not absorb colored ink properly and will result in a poor-quality product. Toner or ink can actually flake off textured paper, too, so caution is important when choosing the right kind of paper for a project. Glossy paper is covered in a finish that allows for sharper, more accurate image reproduction. Each brand of printer has its own specific kind of glossy paper. So when using an Epson printer, a smart designer knows to seek out Epson or another compatible brand paper.

Students printing their own desktop publishing designs have decisions similar to those of major printing operations: What kind of paper should I use? What kind of printer would give me the best quality?

After coming up with the newsletter's name, decide where to place the main article about the results of the survey. Since this will be the main feature of the newsletter, it should have its own headline, which will be in a font size different from the title of the newsletter. If the newsletter is going to contain other articles, consider where to place them in relation to the main article.

When choosing font size, consider what fonts would be most appropriate for the headlines and body text. For the headlines and newsletter title, large display fonts might be most appropriate. For the body text, select a readable font, such as Times New Roman in twelve-point type. Also, decide how many columns the newsletter should have and set the margins. After determining how the content will be laid out in the newsletter, it's time to figure out which images will be included.

MYTHS & FACTS

MYTH
FACT
You have to be a professional with years of experience to do graphic design.
Most graphic design and desktop publishing software is so easy to
use that, with some practice, even a beginner can create designs and
layouts. Of course, learning how to use software applications to create
graphic designs and publishing projects is only the first step. Aspiring
designers can pursue their interest in the art and craft of design and
desktop publishing by taking classes, or even pursuing design in college.

MYTH
FACT
Only Macintosh computers are adequate for graphic design.
Professional graphic designers often work on Macs. However, this
is a matter of preference, not necessity. Both Macs and PCs accom-
modate graphic design and desktop publishing software. In addition,
a lot of today's software is "cross-platform," meaning it can be pur-
chased for both Macs and PCs.

MYTH
The colors of a design will print out exactly as they look when displayed
on the computer monitor.

FACT
Images are displayed on a computer monitor with projected light.
However, when we view a design that has been printed out, we
see it because of reflected light. When we see colors on a piece of
paper, we see the reflection of light that first hits the paper and then
is screened by the colors printed there. The color the eye perceives
from projected light can look different from the color perceived from
reflected light. Designers sometimes have to recheck and then adjust
the percentages of red, green, and blue that make up the chosen hue.

Chapter 3

Images

After organizing content and settling on a typeface, it's time to choose which images will be incorporated into the design. These images can include photographs, illustrations, and visual representations of data such as charts and graphs. When working on the newsletter about the best young adult book series, a student designer can use photos and illustrations as a visual accompaniment to the text. By incorporating images into a design, readers can be shown something while they are also being told something. Illustrations and photos are powerful tools for communication.

Think about the different emotions that illustrations and photographs could convey: fans of Harry Potter and Twilight dressed up as wizards or as vampires, or kids waiting at the library or bookstore for the midnight release of the next book in their favorite series. Images that capture the joy of reading can be added to the newsletter to grab readers' interest. As always, the most important consideration is to make sure that a photo or illustration evokes the right emotion for the project.

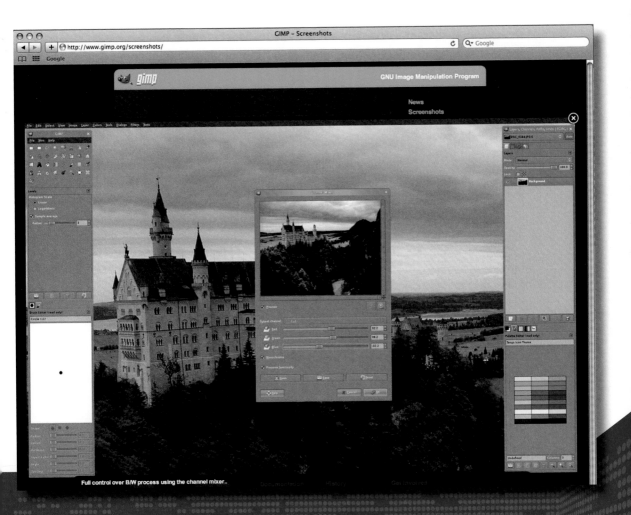

The freely distributed software GIMP (seen here at http://www.gimp.org) allows users to dramatically alter digital photos, such as by cropping the image or adjusting its color balance.

Starting Out

When incorporating images into a design, the design should determine whether they are raster-based images or vector-based images. Raster-based images, also known as bitmap images, reproduce images by rendering them

Zooming in on a raster-based photo on the computer screen will reveal the individual pixels that blend together to form the image.

as pixels on a rectangular grid. Digital photographs are usually formatted as raster-based images.

Vector-based images, meanwhile, are much different from raster-based images. Vector-based images are mathematically precise and are generally used by designers to represent lines, curves, and geometric shapes.

The difference between the two kinds of images is easiest to see when one of each type of image is blown up. If a raster photo is blown up, the individual bits of color that form the image are visible. A vector image, on the other hand, will blow up perfectly to any size. This is because vector images are mathematically computed. The clarity of a digital image is known as its resolution. Because they are mathematically computed, vector-based images always have the same resolution. The resolution of a raster-based image, however, decreases the more a person zooms in on it.

To manipulate raster-based images, many designers use applications such as Adobe Photoshop, Corel Paint Shop Pro, MS Paint, and the open-source design program known as GIMP. Vector-based images are generally created using illustration programs such as CorelDRAW and Adobe Illustrator. Software options are called drawing programs. They include CorelDRAW and Adobe Illustrator.

Digital Photography

When deciding what image or photograph to include in a design, make sure that the photo conveys the point of the design or illustrates the text it accompanies. Let's say that the newsletter about the best young adult book series includes a chart showing how many students voted for each series. The chart shows that Harry Potter wins hands-down. The newsletter designer decides to illustrate a photograph of Harry Potter fans wearing wizard hats.

Professional designers often purchase photographs to use in their design and sometimes hire professional photographers to take pictures specifically for a design. However, doing this costs money. Another option is for the designer to simply take the photographs. Photography is an art, and a

Young designers today can take advantage of the ease of transferring digital shots directly to their computers, without the time-consuming and expensive step of developing the photos.

beginning photographer will need to experiment with close-ups, wide-angle shots, and different angles.

Acquiring Photographs

There are numerous resources available for designers who are looking to acquire images for their designs. Licensed, professionally shot images are known as stock images. A designer has to pay for the right to use these images, and some can be expensive. Two of the biggest stock image agencies are Getty Images and Corbis.

_ □ X

File   Edit   View   Favorites   Tools   Help

DIGITAL CAMERAS

Digital Cameras

A student who wants to get into digital photography can acquire an inexpensive digital camera that is capable of taking high-resolution photos that will print well. It's best to use a camera with at least a seven-megapixel capability. This is a rating that measures how well a camera captures an image. Digital photos should generally have a resolution of at least three hundred dpi, meaning three hundred dots per inch. This is the ideal resolution for printing. Photos or other images used on a Web site should have a resolution of seventy-two dpi. The number of dots per inch determines the resolution of the photo. Photos that have a low resolution will not print (or, in the case of a Web site, display) clearly. Sometimes dpi is also referred to as ppi, or pixels per inch.

When money is an issue, microstock photography agencies such as Shutterstock, which charges a small yearly subscription fee, and Dreamstime are more economical choices. Some Dreamstime photos can be used for as little as twenty cents apiece, or are even free!

Designers may also want to consider using historic photos that are in the public domain. The term "public domain" refers to media that are available for anyone to use. Public domain images are those printed before 1923, or those not under anyone's control. This means that they are not owned by individuals or government or commercial entities. The Library of Congress offers many public domain digital images. For instance, photographs taken by many famous photographers—such as Dorothea Lange, a photographer who documented the Great Depression, and Edward Curtis, a photographer who documented the Western Indian tribes at the turn of the twentieth century—are in the public domain and are available through the Library of Congress. Generally, seventy years must elapse from the date of the author's, photographer's, or artist's death before the work lapses into the public domain.

Sometimes photographs can be found on photo-sharing Web sites such as Flickr.com. Members of Flickr can download up to one hundred

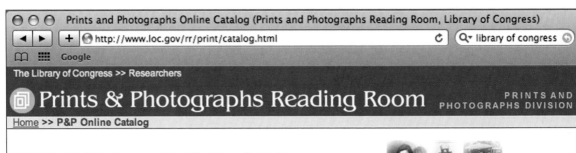

Anyone can use public domain images in their designs. The Library of Congress (http://www.loc.gov) maintains a large online catalog of public domain images.

megabytes worth of photos each month for free or pay a small subscription fee if they want to download more. The photos found on Flickr are mostly contributed by amateur photographers.

When acquiring photographs, it's important that designers read the fine print about copyright. Designers can't simply take photos or illustrations they see in magazines or on the Web. Using an image without permission could violate the copyright of whoever owns the rights to that image: it's important to check whether the photo or illustration is in the public domain.

Sometimes copyrighted material can be used if the designer doesn't stand to make any money from using it. This is known as fair use. The Copyright Act of 1976 lists reasons for claiming fair use, such as criticism, news reporting, and research. The purpose and nature of the use of copyrighted material determines whether or not it can be claimed as fair use. Some of these criteria include whether the copyrighted material is being used for commercial gain or nonprofit educational purposes and how large a portion of the original work is being reproduced.

Manipulating Photos

Enlarging an image beyond the original size shot by the camera may lessen the image's resolution. For this reason, it's a good idea to photograph or download an image a bit larger than the size to be used in a design. This ensures that the image resolution will be fine for the final, printed product. It's good to remember that the higher the resolution a digital image has, the more memory the image file takes up.

The layout of a design will often dictate the size and shape of the images it includes. For instance, the available space in the design might call for a horizontal image or a vertical image. Just as it's important not to lessen an image's resolution by enlarging it beyond its original size, it's also important to keep the height and width of the image proportional. This can help avoid distortion.

When designers want to emphasize one part of a photograph, they can crop the photo. Cropping a photo allows the designer to eliminate distracting details and focus on what's most important. Programs such as Adobe Photoshop allow designers to retouch and resize images easily. When working with multiple images, it's important to name and save the files so that they can be easily organized and accessed.

Digital photos can also be altered by the use of photo effects. For instance, the selective color effect allows a designer to spotlight a single item against a black-and-white background. Color photos can be made mono-tone, meaning they are reduced to one color, or duotone, meaning they are reduced to two colors. Black-and-white photos can be tinted with color, such as sepia, which can give photos an antique effect. One of the simplest and most important ways to manipulate a photo is to adjust its color. If an image seems like it's too red or too green, the color values can be adjusted so that it looks normal. Conversely, if a photo is too dull looking, the colors can be pumped up to make it look more vibrant.

Manipulating Illustrations

All kinds of illustrations can be included in a design. These can range from pen-and-ink drawings that have been converted into digital images with a scanner, to complex technical illustrations. Technical illustrations are precise drawings that are intended to clearly illustrate technical information. These are often created using CAD, or computer-aided design, software.

Illustrations come in one of several different image formats. JPEG (Joint Photographic Experts Group) files are commonly used, as the JPEG file format compresses images. TIFF (tagged image file format) files can't be compressed as much as JPEGs, but they are better at accurately depicting images than JPEGs are. TIFF files are often used for illustrations. GIF (graphic interchange format) files are used for images that will appear on the Internet. GIF files generally contain less information than TIFF files and use prescribed colors that will display on the Internet. As with digital photographs, illustrations can be cropped, resized, and otherwise digitally altered.

TEN GREAT QUESTIONS

TO ASK A GRAPHIC DESIGNER

1. What careers are available in graphic design and desktop publishing?

2. How do I choose which software to buy?

3. How can I determine if a photo is in the public domain?

4. How can I create a balanced design?

5. Where can I acquire special fonts for my computer?

6. How can I figure out if certain colors are complementary?

7. What's the best digital camera to buy for graphic design?

8. How do I fix off-balance color in my photo?

9. How do I make sure that my design doesn't include any trapped space?

10. Is it OK to put some elements outside of the lines in my design grid?

Chapter 4

Layout

nce all of the content for a design has been assembled and the images have been gathered, it's time to lay everything out. The layout of the design will bring everything together into a coherent whole. A layout program, such as Adobe InDesign, can incorporate text, photos, and illustrations. For Web design, layout may be accomplished through code languages such as CSS or HTML, often with the assistance of programs like Adobe Dreamweaver. Let's consider layout in terms of the young adult book series newsletter.

Grids

Grids are two-dimensional frameworks of intersecting vertical and horizontal lines that help organize a layout. Often, designs that incorporate blocks of text, such as newspapers, arrange the text into vertical columns.

Layout programs such as InDesign allow a designer to turn grids on when creating a layout and turn them off after the layout is completed. A

Grids, or two-dimensional frameworks of intersecting lines, can help the designer place design elements in a way that is pleasing to the eye.

single-column layout is one type of grid category. Multiple columns are another type of grid, while rows are horizontal organizing elements.

Balance and Visual Path

Visual flow describes the quality of a design that directs the reader's eyes along a specific path. There are a number of strategies that designers

Professional designers know how to combine images and text for maximum impact. These two-page spreads have been designed to draw the reader's eye across the page.

employ to achieve this, such as positioning text and images in a hierarchy, numbering images, inserting arrows, and the path the viewer's eye should follow.

When designing a newsletter, it's important to keep text placement consistent. This means that all text in the design is placed flush left, flush right, or in the center of the page. Giving different lines of text different alignments will create a sloppy and unfocused design.

The arrangement of blocks of text and empty space on a page determines what the reader will look at first. The higher the placement of a block of text, the more important it is. Text can be linked to an image with a rule or straight line or by overlapping the text with the image itself. Individual words can be emphasized by making them bold or italic or by placing them in a larger font.

One way that designers break up large blocks of text to make them more readable is to create a pull quote. A pull quote (or "drop quote") is an excerpt from the text, enlarged and put in a bold font. Pull quotes are useful for highlighting a main point from the text. Text can be broken up by the use of subheads, or smaller headlines within a main article.

Most designs that include text also have margins, or areas around the outside of the page that are blank. Generally, the horizontal margin at the bottom of the page is larger than the margin at the top of the page. When working on designs that involve page spreads, or two pages that face each other, it's best to make the inside margins thinner than those on the outside. The inside margins of a spread are known as the gutter. For newsletters, a thick margin is generally left at the top of the page for the name of the newsletter and other important information. This area is known as the masthead.

Form, Space, and Trapped Space

Just as designers choose the kind of typeface they're going to use, they can also choose to add empty space to a layout. Adding empty space to

The FedEx logo is one of the most famous uses of negative space in a design. The negative space between the "E" and the "x" creates an arrow pointing forward.

a design can make it less cluttered, as well as simpler, more elegant, and more readable.

In the book *Graphic Design for Non-Designers*, authors Tony Seddon and Jane Waterhouse explain that combining elements in a layout—such as blocks of text, images, and lines and rules—produces new shapes called forms.

Forms are the "positive" part of the layout; space is the "negative" part. So putting too much into the positive space results in a cramped layout, while putting in too much negative space results in a layout that looks empty. The designer, then, must experiment to arrive at a relationship between form and space that achieves a satisfying artistic balance, as well as effective

Computers and software are tools that serve the imagination of designers, who can use these tools to maximize the appeal of the pieces they create.

communication. When doing this, the designer must be careful to avoid trapped space. Trapped space is space that is hemmed in by two or more forms, an effect that may distract from, rather than add to, the overall design. A strong, decisive layout, the authors say, uses distinct contrasts between form and space. A quieter-feeling layout has a more open-form space relationship. By testing different placements of form and space, a designer can hit upon the right look.

Trial and Error

By experimenting with different groupings of forms, designers can figure out how to avoid trapped space and ultimately produce the most effective layout. When viewers look at the design, what will they see first? Is this the element that the designer wants to show first? What is the second thing the viewer will see? Or the third? Would increasing or decreasing the size of certain elements, such as the image and type and headings, change the relationship among those elements to emphasize just the right one? The best design for a desktop publishing project can be discovered.

additive color The color model from which other colors are made by combining red, green, and blue.

asymmetrical The quality of being not balanced, or not the same on both sides. An asymmetrical design has unbalanced type and images.

desktop publishing A term that refers to the act of creating designs and publishing projects on personal computers.

drop cap A large, uppercase letter at the beginning of a paragraph or chapter. Drop caps are used for decorative purposes.

fair use The legal right to reproduce works that are not in the public domain. The terms of fair use are set out in the Copyright Act of 1976.

font A style of typeface.

graphic design The art of communicating visual ideas, images, and messages.

grid A two-dimensional framework of horizontal and vertical lines that organizes a graphic design layout.

hierarchy The principle that establishes how important an element is in a design.

kerning The horizontal spacing between letters.

leading The vertical spacing between lines of text.

pixel A contraction of the words "picture element"; the digital element that composes computer imagery and is sometimes referred to as a dot.

primary colors The basic colors (red, yellow, and blue) used to create other colors.

raster images Digital images that consist of pixels placed on a rectangular grid.

secondary colors Colors that are created by mixing primary colors. When mixed with their adjacent colors on the color wheel, they create the tertiary colors.

serif Decorative headers and footers on letters.

symmetrical The quality of being balanced across a central axis. Symmetrical designs are those in which each side is a mirror image of the other.

tertiary colors Colors that result from mixing primary and secondary colors.

thumbnail sketch A preliminary design drawing.

tone The degree, or gradient, of lightness and darkness in a particular color.

trapped space In a layout, space that is hemmed in by two or more forms. This space does not contribute to the overall design and should be avoided.

vector images Mathematically precise images that are useful for lines, curves, and shapes like polygons.

WYSIWYG What you see is what you get; a term that refers to digital technology that allows designers to create a design on their computer that, when displayed, will closely resemble what it looks like at the printing stage.

American Institute of Graphic Arts (AIGA)
164 Fifth Avenue
New York, NY 10010
(212) 807-1990
Web site: http://www.aiga.org
A nonprofit organization, the AIGA is the oldest professional membership
    graphic design organization in the United States.

Association of Registered Graphic Designers of Ontario (RGD Ontario)
Spadina Avenue, Suite 503
Toronto, ON M5V 2J6
Canada
(888) 274-3668
Web site: http://www.rgdontario.com
This organization represents more than three thousand graphic designers,
    managers, educators, and students. RGD Ontario promotes standards
    and ethics for designers in Ontario, and gives them a unified voice.

Graphic Artists Guild
32 Broadway, Suite 1114
New York, NY 10004
(212) 791-3400
Web site: www.graphicartistsguild.org
The Graphic Artists Guild is dedicated to upholding and maintaining industry
    standards and protecting members against abuses of pay and poor
    work conditions.

Organization of Black Designers (OBD)
300 M Street SW, Suite N-110

Washington, DC 20024
(202) 659-3918
Web site: http://www.obd.org
Created in 1990, the OBD is a multicultural, multidisciplinary organization
    with more than ten thousand members.

Society of Graphic Designers of Canada (GDC)
Art Court 2 Daly Avenue
Ottawa, ON K1N6E2
Canada
(877) 496 4453
Web site: http://www.gdc.net
Since 1956, the GDC has advocated on behalf of Canada's graphic
    designers, promoting high standards of visual design and ethical busi-
    ness practices.

Web Sites

Due to the changing nature of Internet links, Rosen Publishing has developed
an online list of Web sites related to the subject of this book. This site is
updated regularly. Please use this link to access the list:

http://www.rosenlinks.com/dil/gddp

FOR FURTHER READING

Ambrose, Gavin, and Paul Harris. *The Fundamentals of Graphic Design*. West Sussex, England: Worth, 2009.

Ambrose, Gavin, and Paul Harris. *The Visual Dictionary of Graphic Design*. Lausanne, Switzerland: AVA Publishing SA, 2006.

Bodnar, Ethan. *Creative Grab Bag: Creative Solutions for Artists, Illustrators and Designers*. Georgetown, ON, Canada: HW Books, 2009.

Bucher, Stefan G. *The Graphic Eye*. San Francisco, CA: Chronicle Books, 2009.

Carter, David E., ed. *The Big Book of Color in Design*. New York, NY: HarperCollins, 2004.

Carter, David E. *The Little Book of Layouts*. New York, NY: HarperDesign International, 2003.

Crum, Marjorie, and Marcia Layton Taylor. *The Complete Idiot's Guide to Graphic Design*. New York, NY: Penguin Group, 2008.

Edwards, Betty. *Color: A Course in Mastering the Art of Mixing Colors*. New York, NY: Tarcher/Penguin, 2004.

Evamy, Michael. *Graphics Explained: 7 Top Designers, 7 Briefs, 49 Solutions . . . In Their Own Words*. Beverly, MA: Rockport Publishers, Inc., 2009.

Faimon, Peg. *The Designer's Guide to Business and Careers*. Cincinnati, OH: HOW Design Books, 2009.

Heller, Stephen. *Design School Confidential*. Beverly, MA: Rockport Publishers, Inc., 2009.

Heller, Stephen, and Seymour Chast. *Graphic Style: From Victorian to Digital*. New York, NY: Harry Abrams, 2009.

Knight, Carolyn, and Jessica Glaser. *Create Impact with Type, Image & Color*. Mies, Switzerland: Rotovision SA, 2007.

Krause, Jim. *Design Basics Index*. Cincinnati, OH: HOW Design
    Books, 2004.

Lupton, Ellen, Ed. *D.I.Y.: Design It Yourself*. New York, NY: Princeton
    Architectural Press, 2006.

Maneesh, Sethi. *Web Design for Teens*. Boston, MA: Thomson Course
    Technology PTR, 2005.

Millman, Debbie. *How to Think Like a Great Graphic Designer*. New York,
    NY: Allworth Press, 2007.

Seddon, Tony, and Jane Waterhouse. *Graphic Design for Non-Designers*.
    San Francisco, CA: Chronicle Books, 2009.

Smith, Jennifer, Christopher Smith, and Fred Gerantabee. *Adobe
    Creative Suite 4, Design for Dummies*. Hoboken, NJ: Wiley
    Publishing, 2009.

BIBLIOGRAPHY

Crum, Marjorie, and Marcia Layton Taylor. *The Complete Idiot's Guide to Graphic Design*. New York, NY: Penguin Group, 2008.

Goldstein, Howard. Interview with the author. November 21, 2009.

Grinnell, Craig. *The Essential Guide to CSS and HTML Web Design*. Berkeley, CA: Apress, 2007.

Harris, Sylvia. Interview with the author. October 16, 2009.

Lupton, Ellen, ed. *D.I.Y.: Design It Yourself*. New York, NY: Princeton Architectural Press, 2006.

McConnell, Jeffrey, ed. *Computer Graphics Companion*. New York, NY: NPG Nature Publishing, 2002.

Newark, Quentin. *What Is Graphic Design?* Mies, Switzerland: Roto Vision, 2007.

Seddon, Tony, and Jane Waterhouse. *Graphic Design for Non-Designers*. San Francisco, CA: Chronicle Books, 2009.

INDEX

About the Author

Joan Oleck is a writer based in Brooklyn, New York. She has written for publications such as *BusinessWeek*, *International Design*, *Newsday*, and Salon.com.

Photo Credits

Cover (top left), p. 1 (top left), cover (background), interior design, pp. 16, 37 © www.istockphoto.com; cover (second from left), p. 1 (second from left), p. 13 © www.istockphoto.com/Ales Veluscek; cover (top right), p. 1 (top right), p. 18 © www.istockphoto.com/lara Seregni; cover (second from right), p. 1 (second from right), p. 7 © www.istockphoto.com/mumin inan; p. 8 Justin Sullivan/Getty Images; p. 10 © www.istockphoto.com/Steven Allan; p. 19 © www.istockphoto.com/Wojtek Kryczka; p. 24 © www.istockphoto.com/Inga Ivanova; p. 26 Allison Michael Orenstein/The Image Bank/Getty Images; p. 33 © Nicole Russo; p. 34 Lisa Maree Williams/Getty Images; p. 36 JB Reed/Bloomberg/Getty Images.

Designer: Nicole Russo; Photo Researcher: Marty Levick